The
Free Enterprise
Patriot

By JOHN RICKEY

Had the complexity of today's bureaucratic government existed when the War of Independence began, this is how it might have been, with one exception . . . we probably wouldn't have won.

ILLUSTRATED BY JOSEPH ROGERS

FARNSWORTH

August 7, 1776
Wilfred Corners
Independent Colony
of Massachusetts

Cannon Buyer
Continental Congress
Philadelphia
Independent Colony
of Pennsylvania

To whom it may concern:

I strongly favor the action taken by representatives of the Colonies on July 4, 1776. Since I want to do my part to help, I want to know if you could use an extra cannon. I have a small blacksmith shop here in Wilfred Corners which I run myself. I have never made a cannon, but I'm sure I could do it and if need be, I could get some of the men around these parts to help. I would only charge for the metal I put into it plus a little to help my family buy corn meal and meat for the winter.

Please let me know what kind of cannon you want and where you want it, and I'll get started on it right away.

Yours truly,
Andrew Farnsworth
Owner and Proprietor
Farnsworth Blacksmith Shop

Continental Congress

27 August 1776
Philadelphia, Pennsylvania

Andrew Farnsworth
Farnsworth Blacksmith Shop
Wilfred Corners, Massachusetts

In Reply,
Refer to: WXI-344

Dear Mr. Farnsworth:

In order to conduct business affairs with the Continental Congress and the supply agencies of the Colonial Army, it will be necessary for you to complete certain routine forms to help our Weapons Procurement Evaluation Branch (WPEB) evaluate your business and determine whether you qualify as a supplier for the Colonial Army. Naturally, in the interests of security during this period of unrest, the government agencies must insure that its suppliers meet minimum standards of quality and performance. Please fill out the attached forms (provided in triplicate), retain one file copy, and return the other copies along with a statement of the types of weapons manufacture or Army supply on which you wish to bid.

By Authority of
The Continental Congress
and the Articles of Confederation

Robert J. Larkport
Chief, Industrial Affairs Branch
Congress Procurement Office

Encl: Triplicate Forms

FARNSWORTH

September 26, 1776
Wilfred Corners
Independent Colony
of Massachusetts

Robert J. Larkport
Chief, Industrial Affairs Branch
Congress Procurement Office
Philadelphia, Pennsylvania

Dear Mr. Larkport:

I am sorry it took so long to return the forms you sent me. The weather has been very dry and the farmers here are dulling a lot of plowshares on the rocks in the dry soil. So I've been very busy.

What I want to know is whether you could use a cannon if I would make one. There might be something else I could build but I don't know what it is, so just let me know what you want me to do.

Yours truly,
Andrew Farnsworth
Owner and Proprietor
Farnsworth Blacksmith
Shop

Continental Congress

October 16, 1776
Philadelphia, Pennsylvania

Andrew Farnsworth
Farnsworth Blacksmith Shop
Wilfred Corners, Massachusetts

Dear Mr. Farnsworth:

In reply,
Refer to: WX2-4456

The enclosed bidders forms were incorrectly forwarded to this office. The Industrial Affairs Branch of the Congress Procurement Office is responsible for initial business-government contracts. As a weapons supply industry, the Industrial Questionnaire you sent this office should be directed to the following:

Chief, Industrial Qualification Board
Weapons Procurement Evaluation Branch (WPEB)
Bureau of Ordnance
Headquarters, Colonial Army
Philadelphia,
Home of the Continental Congress

If we can be of additional service, please contact us.

By Authority of
The Continental Congress
and the Articles of Confederation

Horace Marks

Horace Marks
Asst. Chief, Industrial Affairs Branch
Congress Procurement Office

HM:wx
Enc: Three Forms (completed)

FARNSWORTH

November 1, 1776
Wilfred Corners
Independent Colony
of Massachusetts

Chief, Industrial Qualification Board
Weapons Procurement Evaluation Branch (WPEB)
Bureau of Ordnance
Headquarters, Colonial Army
Philadelphia, Pennsylvania

Dear Sir:

I sent these forms to the wrong office and they sent them back and said to send them to you. I am a blacksmith and would like to build a cannon for the Colonial Army. Please tell me what kind of cannon you need most and I will get right to work on it. It is winter now and other work is slack.

Yours truly,
Andrew Farnsworth
Owner and Proprietor
Farnsworth Blacksmith Shop

Colonial Army

November 22, 1776
Philadelphia, Pennsylvania

Andrew Farnsworth
Owner & Proprietor
Farnsworth Blacksmith Shop
Wilfred Corners, Massachusetts

In Reply,
Refer to: MW-897

Dear Mr. Farnsworth:

The Bidders Qualification Forms which you completed and forwarded to this office November 1, 1776 have been received. Initial review of your qualifications indicates that you have no previous experience in cannon design and construction under Colonial Army specifications. Also, our records reveal no other blacksmith shops among those on the qualified cannon suppliers list. Unless you can provide evidence of qualification beyond that supplied on previously submitted documents, the review of your capability for this assignment cannot be continued.

I might add that we carry a number of industries listed as blacksmith shops on our bidders list for "Horses, Shoeing in the Field." Should the war come through your village and you be on the approved contractors list for this vital assignment, you would be eligible to compete with other nearby blacksmiths for these contracts. In case you are interested, I am enclosing blank Bidders Qualification Forms (in triplicate).

By Order of the Commanding Officer

Winfield Jenkins

Winfield Jenkins, GS-11
Industrial Qualification Board
Weapons Procurement Evaluation Branch
Bureau of Ordnance   (WPEB)
Headquarters, Colonial Army
Philadelphia, Pennsylvania

WJ:rst
Enc: 3 Bidders Qualification Forms

FARNSWORTH BLACKSMITH SHOP
and
CANNON WORKS

December 19, 1776
Wilfred Corners
Independent Colony
of Massachusetts

Winfield Jenkins, GS-11
Industrial Qualification Board
Weapons Procurement Evaluation Branch (WPEB)
Bureau of Ordnance
Headquarters, Colonial Army
Philadelphia, Pennsylvania

Dear Mr. Jenkins:

I thank you for the new Bidders Qualification Forms for "Horses, Shoeing in the Field." I am sorry, but if the war gets any place close to Wilfred Corners, I will pack up my family and make a dash for the Canadian border. It therefore seems unnecessary to complete the forms for qualification in this area of supply.

I would still like to build a cannon. Since I last wrote you and sent the forms, I had occasion to ride over to Concord for some corn meal and two seal skin pelts for the bellows on my forge. While there, I had an opportunity to observe a British Cannon that had been used in the recent fighting in that area. I am now sure I could build a cannon. It is nothing but a long hollow tube with some bands around it and closed at one end. I have an idea for a sight similar to one I use on my squirrel rifle, and I'll bet that would improve the markmanship of the cannoneers.

Seeing a real cannon has so enthused me

that I have changed the name of my business to "Farnsworth Blacksmith Shop & Cannon Works." I would not have been able to spend so much time on this but the winter has been hard, and I've had very little regular blacksmith business.

Yours truly,
Andrew Farnsworth
Owner & Proprietor
Farnsworth Blacksmith Shop
& Cannon Works

Colonial Army

January 11, 1777
Philadelphia, Pennsylvania

Andrew Farnsworth
Owner & Proprietor
Farnsworth Blacksmith Shop   In Reply,
    & Cannon Works   Refer to: MW-7605
Wilfred Corners, Massachusetts

Dear Mr. Farnsworth:

I am pleased to advise you that the additional research and study
in cannon design pointed out in your recent letter, plus the alter-
ation of company orientation as evidenced by the new name of your
organization has enabled us to reopen our investigation of your
qualifications for bidding on the design and production of cannons
for the Colonial Army.

I must caution you in regard to the suggested invention of a new
device for improving the accuracy of cannoneers. After initial
submission of a Bidders Qualification Form to this office, all
rights to all inventions of your company become the property of
the Colonial Army and the Continental Congress.

By Order of the Commanding Officer

Winfield Jenkins

Winfield Jenkins, GS-11
Industrial Qualification Board
Weapons Procurement Evaluation Branch
                                    (WPEB)

Bureau of Ordnance
Headquarters, Colonial Army
Philadelphia, Pennsylvania

Colonial Army

January 19, 1777
Philadelphia, Pennsylvania

Andrew Farnsworth
Owner & Proprietor
Farnsworth Blacksmith Shop
   & Cannon Works
Wilfred Corners, Massachusetts

In Reply,
Refer to: WPB-D-2419

Dear Mr. Farnsworth:

Enclosed you find Military Equipment Specification Number 891 outlining the characteristics of a cannon to be produced for the Colonial Army. As a manufacturer who has met the requirements of the Industrial Qualification Branch, your company is authorized to bid for the production of the following named item.

Category	Description
cannon weapons system (mobile)	Three Inch Muzzle;
	Load Capability, 12 pound shot;
	Range Capability, 500 yards;
	Must be light enough for five men to transport two miles in one day without exhaustion.

Initial contract will be for prototype. Expect production order competition to follow.

Bids for this equipment will be received no later than March 1, 1777.

By Order of the Commanding Officer

Conrad Scott

Conrad Scott, GS-14
Weapons Procurement Board
Bureau of Ordnance
Headquarters, Colonial Army
Philadelphia, Pennsylvania

CS:gh

FARNSWORTH
and
Cooper cannon and *Carriage Co.*

February 20, 1777
Wilfred Corners
Independent Colony
of Massachusetts

Conrad Scott, GS-14
Weapons Procurement Board
Bureau of Ordnance
Headquarters, Colonial Army
Philadelphia, Pennsylvania

Dear Mr. Scott:

  With this letter I am sending you my bid for doing the cannon needed by the Colonial Army. Because you need a cannon on wheels, I have sold half my blacksmith shop to Leonard Cooper who has some experience in building wagons. He sold me half of his barn which is where he makes wagons. Since we didn't have any money, we made the half-prices the same so that it didn't cost anybody anything.

  We are going right to work on the cannon you asked for. It will be just like you said in the description, and we believe we can have it done in six weeks. We didn't understand what you meant by prototype so we are not going to be able to start on it right away until you explain what it is because we might do something wrong. Send a letter back right away explaining that part.

  The cannon we are making will look like the picture we have drawn. The men who pull the cannon the two miles every day will be able to get

in between the bars on the shaft. You will notice
we have fixed this rather simple so that if they
want to advance they just face the right of the
picture and push, and if they want to retreat they
face the left and pull. We are going to make it
easier to push than to pull so that iw will be easier
to advance than retreat. That will probably be
another advantage of our cannon...soldier morale.

Incidently, you didn't say what color you
wanted the wheels. We are using the wheels off of
Cooper's old log wagon and they are red. If that is
O. K., we won't paint them again. That way we will
cut the cost.

The cost will be about $400, we figure. We
think that will be a good price.

Please let us know about that prototype thing,
and where you want us to deliver the cannon when we
get done with it.

Sincerely,
Andrew Farnsworth
President
Farnsworth & Cooper
Cannon & Carriage Company

Colonial Army

March 11, 1777
Philadelphia, Pennsylvania

Andrew Farnsworth
President
Farnsworth & Cooper Cannon &
   Carriage Company
Wilfred Corners, Massachusetts

In Reply:
Refer to: WPB-O-420

Dear Mr. Farnsworth:

I just got your letter today. Stop work on the cannon immediately. You do not have a contract yet. We cannot make payment for work done on a government contract before the contract is let.

As I said in my previous letter, we will review your proposal for a prototype of the cannon you expect to build (and I hope, have not yet completed). A prototype means the first of a kind. In other words, the first cannon you build, unfortunately, the one you are building.

Please do not do any more work on your cannon until you hear from this office concerning the outcome of the proposal evaluation.

By Order of the Commanding Officer

Conrad Scott

Conrad Scott, GS-14
Weapons Procurement Board
Bureau of Ordnance
Headquarters, Colonial Army
Philadelphia, Pennsylvania

CS:gh

17

FARNSWORTH
and
Cooper cannon and *Carriage Co.*

March 30, 1777
Wilfred Corners
Independent Colony
of Massachusetts

Conrad Scott, GS-14
Weapons Procurement Board
Bureau of Ordnance
Headquarters, Colonial Army
Philadelphia, Pennsylvania

Dear Mr. Scott:

I'm sure sorry you made us stop working on our cannon because we were making good progress with it. Now spring plowing is almost here and I will be busy with plowshare sharpening. Leonard Cooper is helping Vance Putman build a sawmill on Benshire Creek north of town, so we won't be able to work on the cannon for several weeks.

However, if your letter comes telling us to start work, we'll be at it every spare moment. I hope our tight schedule won't interfere with your decision to have us build the cannon because we sure are anxious.

Sincerely,
Andrew Farnsworth
President
Farnsworth & Cooper Cannon &
Carriage Company

P. S. We put up a sign outside my shop showing our new name, but folks around still know to bring their plowshares here for sharpening.

Colonial Army

July 14, 1777
Philadelphia, Pennsylvania

Andrew Farnsworth
President
Farnsworth & Cooper Cannon
    & Carriage Company
Wilfred Corners, Massachusetts

In Reply,
Refer to: WPO-44902

Dear Mr. Farnsworth:

We are pleased to advise you that your company has been selected as one of four to build a 52C-3 prototype cannon.

Terms of the contract are cost of materials plus a fixed fee of 5%. On the basis of your proposed cost, the target price will be $400 with a profit fee of $20. You are cautioned to keep exact records of supplies purchased and time expended for the production of this unit as auditors of the Government Accounting Office will review expenditures prior to contract completion and payment. Such promotional expenditures as the cost of the sign you mentioned outside your plant are not allowable as costs chargeable against government contracts. Work performed prior to the date of this contract is considered part of the cost of proposal and will be discounted by the GAO.

You are cautioned that the product you are building has a security classification of secret and must be kept from the view of unauthorized persons at all times.

During the course of this contract, your designated contracting officer is:

Major Hollis Corby
Contracting Officer
J2C-3 Weapons Systems
Weapons Procurement Branch
Headquarters, Colonial Army
Philadelphia, Pennsylvania

By Order of the Commanding Officer

Major Hollis Corby
Contracting Officer
J2C-3 Weapons Systems
Weapons Procurement Branch
Headquarters, Colonial Army
Philadelphia, Pennsylvania

HC:bj

Colonial Army

July 15, 1777
Philadelphia, Pennsylvania

Andrew Farnsworth
President
Farnsworth & Cooper Cannon
   & Carriage Company
Wilfred Corners, Massachusetts

In Reply,
Refer to: SRA 7732

Dear Mr. Farnsworth:

As a weapons system prime contractor to the Colonial Army of the Continental Congress, you are herein advised of government regulations that apply to such contractors.

1. Weapons System contractors will maintain such security as necessary to prevent weapons developments from falling into unauthorized hands. Such guards as necessary to protect the weapons manufacturing area will be hired. Fences and walls may be constructed to assist in carrying out this requirement. All employees will complete Security Form No. 287 and receive clearance from the Colonial Bureau of Investigation prior to being assigned to work on this contract.

2. In order to fulfill the objectives which led to the establishment of the Small Business Administration, you are directed to subcontract at least 20% of this contract to qualified small businesses in your area.

3. The Fair Employment Practices Commission requires that you, as a federal contractor, provide equal employment opportunities to all. No person is to be denied employment for reasons of race, creed, color or nation of origin.

4. The federal postal officials have advised this office the regulations concerning proper use of the mails have not been followed in past correspondence with the government of the Colonies. Use of the address ''Independent Colony of Massachusetts'' as used in past correspondence must cease and the authorized postal address ''Massachusetts'' is to be used in the future on all correspondence of your company, whether with federal offices or with civilian customers.

5. An authorized representative of this office is being assigned to your facility to supervice production under this contract to assure that all terms of the contract are met. This representative is to be assigned an office in your plant equal in size and degree of improvement to that of your program director.

6. A weapons development and procurement inspection team from the New England Sub-District of the Weapons Procurement Branch will visit your facility from August 1 through August 5 to insure that these contract terms are being complied with.

By Order of the Commanding Officer
Major Hollis Corby
J2C-3 Weapons Systems
Weapons Procurement Branch
Headquarters, Colonial Army
Philadelphia, Pennsylvania

FARNSWORTH
and
Cooper cannon and *Carriage Co.*

September 19, 1777
Wilfred Corners,
Massachusetts

Major Hollis Corby
Contracting Officer
T2C-3 Weapons Systems
Weapons Procurement Branch
Headquarters, Colonial Army
Philadelphia, Pennsylvania

Dear Major Corby,

      I am sorry I didn't write you sooner to
thank you for letting us have the contract to build
the cannon, but the day after we got your letter saying we could build it, we got your other letter explaining some things we had to do before we could
get started. It has taken all our time, almost, to
get these things done and we still haven't been able
to do any more work on the cannon.

      Leonard and I spent the first week after we
got your letter cutting saplings in Haynes Woods to
make a fence around his barn and my blacksmith shop.
We planned to have Ed Crank guard one place while we
worked at the other, but an indian by the name of
Corn-In-The-Woods came by and wanted to work too. We
told him we didn't need him, but he went to your
authorized representative, Captain Hawkins (he got
here the day after your letter) and claimed we'd
better hire him so we've got him watching the black-

smith shop and Ed out at the barn. They haven't found anyone wanting in except some of our regular customers. This is making our customers kind of mad, but we don't know what to do about it. Moss Green who has had me sharpen his scythe for almost ten years now said he wasn't going to wait for me to solve this problem and he took his scythe down to West Concord. It's about a days ride each way, but I guess he still got it done before I could have gotten to it.

Since we have to give 20% of our business to someone else, we decided not to use Leonard's old log wagon wheels. Instead, we are going to buy two new wheels which Charlie Baxter just got into his hardware store.

Getting back to your authorized represent-ative, we're working on getting him fixed up now. We didn't have any office for him but he said con-tractors are expected to provide office facilities equal to those of the Program Director. We didn't have a Program Director for him to have an office like. So I made myself Program Director. I don't have an office, but Captain Hawkins said Program Directors should have one. So I borrowed some money at 7% interest from Roger Harms who owns the big sugar grove north of town and built myself one. Then I had to go borrow some more to build one like it for Captain Hawkins. We're still working on that because we had to take down the security fence we built and move it to make room for the new offices so that set us back some.

The inspection team came like you said they would. They stayed down at Farley's Tavern. Captain Hawkins said that normally a weapons system contractor picks up the bill for a visit like this. We decided we couldn't do that but the team leader said they couldn't make up their minds whether we were meeting the requirements of our contract. Captain Hawkins said that meant we should pick up the bill or we'd lose our contract so we borrowed some more money from Roger Harms. The inspection team said they had reviewed our activity and had decided we qualified after all. One thing most folks around here are saying is that those inspection folks sure do seem to enjoy their work. They all seemed to have a good time here.

We are going to have to wait until we get word on our security clearances before we can start on the cannon. The guards we hired won't let us in until we get them. I tried to get inside to get some tools to help in building the offices and they wouldn't even let me in for that. I sure wish we could get in because I could do some work for my regular customers while we're waiting.

Let us know what we should do next cause we're awful anxious to get started on that cannon.

Sincerely,
Andrew Farnsworth
President and Program Director,
T2C-3
Farnsworth & Cooper Cannon
& Carriage Company

Copy to Captain Hawkins

FARNSWORTH
and
Cooper cannon and *Carriage Co.*

Major Hollis Corby
Contracting Officer
T2C-3 Weapons Systems
Weapons Procurement Branch
Headquarters, Colonial Army
Philadelphia, Pennsylvania

November 17, 1777
Wilfred Corners,
Massachusetts

Dear Major Corby,

     We got started on the cannon today. We would have started last week when the letter came from the Security Branch saying we were authorized to enter the security area, but early in October we had a bad wind storm that blew away part of the roof here at the blacksmith shop. We've been working on that until last night, but we started on the cannon first thing this morning.

     Leonard and I are running the forge and we hired help to cut wood and haul it here to keep the fire up. We hired another Indian named "Red Runner," a Quaker from over at Kerbysville, a drunk named Mose (I don't think he has a last name or maybe he's forgotten it) from here in Wilfred Corners, and a one legged man who came by called Mark Crossfield. We thought that would meet all the regulations about being fair to any folks who want to work on cannons. The one legged fellow can't do any wood cutting or hauling so he guards the wood pile in Evans pasture across the road.

     You might wonder about why we are piling

our wood so far away. We were going to have the help bring it in and stack it right next to the forge, but Ed Crank, the guard here, said our wood-cutters didn't have any clearance to enter a defense plant, so they stack it over across the road and Leonard and I shut down the forge every hour and go carry in some more wood. We weren't going to guard the wood, but Ed said it was government property and should be guarded and besides, the one legged fellow would show the government we have good business practices because we hire the handicapped.

We melted down about twenty pounds of iron today and at this rate, we should have the barrel of the cannon done in about four weeks. We've been out gathering scrap iron from around town while we were waiting for our security clearance. People around here appreciated us cleaning up the town that way. They're mighty proud to have a defense industry like ours here in Wilfred Corners, but Mayor Carter said that defense industries don't pay as much taxes, he'd heard, so he and the town council raised the taxes on my house to make up for any loss they might have.

Captain Hawkins has been coming over to my house for lunch. He says defense industries should have eating facilities for the Contracting Officer.

Sincerely,
Andrew Farnsworth
President and Program Director,
T2C-3
Farnsworth & Cooper Cannon
& Carriage Company

Copy to Captain Hawkins

Colonial Army

19 January 1778
Philadelphia, Pennsylvania

Andrew Farnsworth
President
Farnsworth & Cooper Cannon
    & Carriage Company   In Reply,
Wilfred Corners, Massachusetts Refer to: SRG 9922

Dear Mr. Farnsworth:

With reference to raw material acquisition mentioned in your letter of 17 November 1777, you are advised that under Public Law 6344, defense contractors are authorized to utilize raw materials stockpiled by the Government in order to reduce surplusses that have been accumulated therein. Paragraph 19A of Public Law 6344 directs defense contractors to purchase at least 78% of all iron used in the production of goods and equipment for the Colonial Government from surplus stocks. Iron stocks stockpiled nearest Wilfred Corners are located at Colonial Army Storage Depot, Building 7, Village of Springfield, Massachusetts.

As a defense contractor on 52C-3 Weapons Systems for the Colonial Army, you are advised that use of scrap materials is acceptable for such units up to a maximum of 22% of total weight. All additional iron weight is to be made up of Government surplus iron stocks. You are hereby authorized to purchase no more than 550 pounds or no less than 435 pounds of iron from the

Springfield Depot. Failure to meet this requirement will disqualify the prototype cannon being constructed by your company.

By Order of the Commanding Officer
Major Hollis Corby
Contracting Officer
52C-3 Weapons Systems
Weapons Procurement Branch
Headquarters, Colonial Army
Philadelphia, Pennsylvania

HC:jb

cc to: Captain Earl Hawkins
Plant Representative
52C-3 Contracts

FARNSWORTH
and
Cooper cannon and Carriage Co.

February 19, 1778
Wilfred Corners,
Massachusetts

Major Hollis Corby
Contracting Officer
T2C-3 Weapons Systems
Weapons Procurement Branch
Headquarters, Colonial Army
Philadelphia, Pennsylvania

Dear Major Corby,

    Although we are having one of the hardest winters we ever had, I'm still working on the cannon. Leonard hasn't been able to help on it because of his frostbite.

    Leonard and I made a trip to your Springfield Iron Depot after we got your letter. The first time we went down we didn't have any government surplus purchase authorization papers, but the man you have running the Depot got us some and helped us fill them out. We could have gotten the iron then, but we had to come back to Wilfred Corners and get the Contracting Officer's Representative's signature.

    We went back to Springfield the next day, but after we got the iron loaded on Leonard's wagon, it began to snow and blow and Leonard's bay mares couldn't pull the wagon through the drifts. We left the wagon and rode the mares back to Wilfred Corners. We'd been out in the cold all night by the time we got back. Leonard's horse stumbled as we crossed

Limestone Creek and he fell through the ice, but the water wasn't very deep. Just the same, he got pretty wet, and by the time we got home, Leonard's right hand and his ears and both feet were frozen and he's still in bed. It sure took a lot out of him.

Roscoe Trotter loaned me his big bobsled the next day and I drove back down to the wagon and got the iron we'd bought. We'll have to go pick up the wagon in the spring.

Anyway, I'm working as best I can, but without Leonard to help, it is going to be slow. I'd hire someone to give me a hand until Leonard gets on his feet, but we had to borrow the $400 to buy the iron from Moss Harris who runs the Kingby Toll Road and folks are getting so they won't let me have anymore money on loan.

Sincerely,
Andrew Farnsworth
President & Program Director,
T2C-3
Farnsworth & Cooper Cannon
& Carriage Company

Copy to Captain Hawkins

FARNSWORTH
and
Cooper cannon and *Carriage Co.*

June 5, 1778
Wilfred Corners,
Massachusetts

Major Hollis Corby
Contracting Officer
T2C-3 Weapons Systems
Weapons Procurement Branch
Headquarters, Colonial Army
Philadelphia, Pennsylvania

Dear Major Corby,

Leonard finally got so he could work and began helping me last week.

We poured the last 15 pounds of iron into the barrel mold on Monday and took the mold form off on Wednesday. Boy, she sure looks good. Folks in town want to come in to see it, but Ed Crank, the

guard, said we couldn't let them.

We did throw out the mold forms and every-one was pretty interested in those.

We poured two cannon balls three inches across from some extra iron we had in the forge. We wanted to drop them in the barrel, but they wouldn't go in. I guess the heat slightly shrunk our round form. We think we can grind it out to the right size, but it will sure be a lot of work.

Leonard is working on the carriage now and I'm trying to grind out the barrel. We'll let you know if we have any trouble.

Sincerely,
Andrew Farnsworth
President & Program Director,
T2C-3
Farnsworth & Cooper Cannon &
Carriage Company

Copy to Captain Hawkins

Colonial Army

22 September 1718
Philadelphia, Pennsylvania

Andrew Farnsworth
President
Farnsworth & Cooper Cannon
    & Carriage Company   In Reply,
Wilfred Corners, Massachusetts   Refer to: SRA 16696

Dear Mr. Farnsworth:

You are not authorized to release your tooling for a
Government Contract Weapons System. You must retrieve
the cannon forms you set outside and store them until
your weapons system is phased out of Government inven-
tory as obsolete. Besides, the forms for your cannon
are classified. Defense contractors must give tools
which might reveal weapons system technology the same
protection as the weapon. You are directed to provide
proper security safeguards for this tooling, immediately.

Regarding the apparent shrinkage of the bore of your
cannon, you must meet the three inch specifications
outlined in your contract. A quantity of Government
Specification Cannon Balls (three inch) is being ship-
ped for testing with your cannon to insure compliance.

                    By Order of the Commanding Officer
                    Major Hollis Corby
                    Contracting Officer
                    52C-3 Weapons Systems
                    Weapons Procurement Branch
                    Headquarters, Colonial Army
                    Philadelphia, Pennsylvania
HC:jb

cc to: Captain Earl Hawkins
        Plant Representative
        52C-3 Contracts

FARNSWORTH
and
Cooper cannon and Carriage Co.

December 10, 1778
Wilfred Corners
Massachusetts

Major Hollis Corby
Contracting Officer
T2C-3 Weapons Systems
Weapons Procurement Branch
Headquarters, Colonial Army
Philadelphia, Pennsylvania.

Dear Major Corby,

Guess it is time I brought you up to date on our progress on the cannon.

After your letter came, Leonard and I cut some more saplings and made a fence around the yard alongside my house. Then we moved the cannon forms into the yard. We boarded the windows on that side of the house and locked the gate. I think they'll be protected there.

My wife, Patience, is pretty mad about boarding up the windows of the house. You see, I boarded up the windows on the other side last year so the house would be part of the wall around the wood for the forge. Now we don't have any windows at all and we have to burn a lamp all the time.

We haven't received the cannon ball shipment yet. Meanwhile, Leonard is working on the cannon carriage and I've worked out a horse drawn cannon reamer. I set the cannon upright in the ground and the horse walks around it. We change horses twice a day so we ream the cannon around the clock. I get up every hour or so during the night to make sure Hugo (that's the horse we've been working nights) is still walking.

  Captain Hawkins has moved in with us now. He said since he was taking all his meals at our house it would be easier if he lived there. We moved his office into the attic for the winter so he doesn't need to get out in the cold.

    Sincerely,

    Andrew Farnsworth

    President & Program Director,

        T2C-3

    Farnsworth & Cooper Cannon

      & Carriage Company

Copy to Captain Hawkins

Colonial Army

10 March 1779
Philadelphia, Pennsylvania

Andrew Farnsworth
President
Farnsworth & Cooper Cannon & Carriage Company
Wilfred Corners, Massachusetts

Dear Mr. Farnsworth:

The Patents Department of the Colonial Army is interested in the device developed by your company under government contract for the purpose of reaming cannon barrels. You are instructed to submit drawings of this device for registration. In recognition of your part in the development of the cannon reamer, patent royalties as appropriate under government held patents will not be levied against your current contract.

Future cannon contracts involving use of this device will, of course, include a negotiated patent royalty clause.

By Order of the Commanding Officer
Major Hollis Corby
Contracting Officer
F2C-3 Weapons Systems
Weapons Procurement Branch
Headquarters, Colonial Army
Philadelphia, Pennsylvania

HC:jb

cc to: Captain Earl Hawkins
Plant Representative
F2C-3 Contracts

FARNSWORTH
and
Cooper cannon and *Carriage Co.*

Major Hollis Corby
Contracting Officer
T2C-3 Weapons Systems
Weapons Procurement Branch
Headquarters, Colonial Army
Philadelphia, Pennsylvania

June 9, 1779
Wilfred Corners
Massachusetts

Dear Major Corby,

The cannon ball shipment you sent arrived day before yesterday, just after we finished reaming the cannon to the three inch bore. The crate was marked, "Balls, Cannon, Specification 97864, 3-inch, Colonial Army," but we measured the balls and they ranged from 2 1/2 to 4 1/4 inches in diameter. We found ten that were about three inches, so we'll be able to test our cannon with them.

Leonard finished the carriage last week. It turned out real well. We mounted a heavy log on it and hired some local boys to pull it around for us to see how far they could go in a day. The first day they went four miles and the second day two and a half, but the first day they were going down hill quite a bit. So I guess we'll average out about what you asked for or a little better.

We've moved the carriage into the shop and removed the log and we'll mount the cannon tomorrow.

We had a little problem the last night we reamed the cannon barrel. Some kids were throwing stones over our security fence that evening and one fell into the barrel. During the night it worked into the reamer and gouged a little groove from the top to the bottom around the cannon, but it doesn't look like it will hurt anything.

Sincerely,
Andrew Farnsworth
President & Project Officer,
T2C-3
Farnsworth & Cooper Cannon
& Carriage Company

Copy to Captain Hawkins

Colonial Army

1 August 1779
Philadelphia, Pennsylvania

Andrew Farnsworth
President
Farnsworth & Cooper Cannon
    & Carriage Company
Wilfred Corners, Massachusetts

In Reply,
Refer to: SRA 217-516

Dear Mr. Farnsworth:

Our technical staff has been consulted with reference to the damaging grooves you have cut into the barrel of your cannon. They advise me that this will not be satisfactory and that the barrel must be perfectly smooth. Although it is not known just what effect this groove might have if the cannon was fired, our experts suspect it has weakened the entire structure and that it would be hazardous to fire.

We will have an inspection team in Massachusetts next month and they will examine the cannon to determine if it is repairable. Meanwhile, do not proceed with testing.

There is considerable concern here about the rather haphazard manufacturing techniques used by your concern as exemplified by your negligence in allowing this damage to occur. As provided in subparagraph H, paragraph 24, Amendment 7 of Public Law 928, no payment will be made under your contract if the cannon is found to be irrepairable.

By Order of the Commanding Officer
Major Hollis Corby
Contracting Officer
52C-3 Weapons Systems
Weapons Procurement Branch
Headquarters, Colonial Army
Philadelphia, Pennsylvania

HC:jb

cc to: Captain Earl Hawkins
Plant Representative
52C-3 Contracts

FARNSWORTH
and
Cooper cannon and *Carriage Co.*

October 3, 1779
Wilfred Corners,
Massachusetts

Major Hollis Corby
Contracting Officer
T2C-3 Weapons Systems
Weapons Procurement Branch
Headquarters, Colonial Army
Philadelphia, Pennsylvania

Dear Major Corby,

I am sorry your letter instructing us not to do anything with the cannon came so late as we have already tested up all the cannon balls you sent us. You will be happy to hear that the cannon didn't blow up or anything.

But those grooves did seem to change the cannon quite a bit.

To begin with, we mounted the cannon on the carriage in our shop and she fit on there perfect. Then, in the middle of the night to protect security on it, we hitched up Hugo (that's my horse) and pulled it out to the woods along Feather Creek about 20 miles out of town. There's a valley out there where no one lives so we thought that'd be a good place to try her out.

We got it in place about eight in the morning, all staked down and aimed alongside a clump of trees at a place in the creek bed where we thought the shell would land. We watched some cannons being fired when we were kids during the French and Indian

War so we were pretty sure how it would work. Captain
Hawkins rode out in the morning to watch and he'd
seen a cannon fired down in Hartford about a year ago.

Leonard poured in the powder and I dropped
in the cannon ball and tamped it down good. Then we
tied Leonard's flintlock musket across the barrel
and tied a string to the trigger. We got off behind
a rock about twenty feet away and pulled the string.

The cannon went off just fine and sounded
good, but we couldn't see where the cannon ball hit.
We spent about an hour down in the creek bed looking
for the ball when Whippoorwill Green, an old hermit,
came walking up carrying our cannon ball and wanted
to know what we thought we were doing. He said he'd
been doing his morning chores in his cabin on the
other side of the valley about a mile and a quarter
away when our cannon ball smashed into a wheelbarrow
in his garden. We couldn't understand how it got
clear over there, but he had it and was so insistent

that we pay for his wheelbarrow that we figured some-
how it did.

     The cannon ball hadn't changed much, but
it did have some marks on it that weren't there before. We finally figured out they were made by the
grooves on the inside of our cannon.

     Anyway, we moved the cannon a little so it
wouldn't shoot anymore shot into Whippoorwill's
garden and loaded her up again. Since Whippoorwill
had already seen what we were doing, we couldn't
very well make him leave, so he stayed to watch.

     We fired her again and watched up on the
opposite ridge and sure enough, about a second after
we shot it off, we saw the cannon ball smash against
a pile of stones over there.

     By the time we'd fired all the cannon balls
that would fit the barrel, it was getting dark. We
were getting pretty good at aiming it and could pick
out a bush on the far ridge about a mile away and hit

it almost every time. That cannon sure does make those cannon balls go straight.

We told Whippoorwill not to mention what he'd seen to anybody, and he agreed not to. He said he hadn't seen anyone in a little over two years, so he didn't figure to have too much trouble keeping our secret.

We pulled the cannon back into town during the night, and the next day was Sunday and your letter came today.

Professor Milter, who teaches the children here in Wilfred Corners, heard about what had happened when we fired our cannon. He said that surely the gouged-out marks in our cannon had something to do with the way the cannon works and that he was intending to do some experimenting with that very thing some day. He was surprised at how we'd happened onto his invention.

I'm sorry we didn't wait until your inspection team got here, but since we didn't seem to hurt the cannon any by shooting it, they'll still be able to look it over all right.

Sincerely,
Andrew Farnsworth
President and Project Officer,
T2C-3
Farnsworth & Cooper Cannon
& Carriage Company

Copy to Captain Hawkins

FARNSWORTH
and
Cooper cannon and Carriage Co.

Major Hollis Corby
Contracting Officer
T2C-3 Weapons Systems
Weapons Procurement Branch
Headquarters, Colonial Army
Philadelphia, Pennsylvania

December 8, 1779
Wilfred Corners,
Massachusetts

Dear Major Corby,

Your inspection team arrived a week ago to check our cannon. They left last night. We had a cold snap and they didn't think we ought to try going out into the country to fire the cannon so they just inspected it and talked to Whippoorwill Green, the hermit, about the tests we had last fall. They thought everything seemed all right and said they would say so in their report to you.

Captain Hawkins was very helpful during their visit. He took them around town and entertained them for us in the evening. Leonard and I couldn't be with them much as we've been clerking down at the grocery store nights to get some money to pay interest on our loans. Then, of course, we had to pay boarding down at the hotel for the inspection team and that took some extra money, too.

We had trouble arranging for them to see Whippoorwill. He never comes to town and they said it was too cold to go out to his place, but that they had to interview him as an unbiased witness to our tests. I rode out to get him on Tuesday, but he

47

wouldn't come back with me. I had to get him so when I got back to town, I made up a story about him shooting at me and Sheriff Larson here in Wilfred Corners went out and arrested him and brought him in. He charged me with false arrest and I'm in jail now for 30 days, so I'm not able to do anymore on our cannon for a while. Leonard is working at the store full time to help pay for food for his family and mine while I'm in jail so he can't work on the cannon either.

While I'm here, I'm working on the design for the cannon sight and we should be able to get right to work on that next month.

Let us know what we should do next as I think we're about ready to deliver our cannon to the Army. Where should we send it?

Sincerely,

Andrew Farnsworth

President and Project Officer,

T2C-3

Farnsworth & Cooper Cannon &

Carriage Company

Copy to Captain Hawkins

Colonial Army

Andrew Farnsworth
President
Farnsworth & Cooper Cannon
    & Carriage Company
Wilfred Corners, Massachusetts

In Reply,
Refer to: SRC
8113-670

Dear Mr. Farnsworth:

You are advised that 52C-3 Weapons Systems Evaluation
Tests at the Salem Ordnance Plant, Weapons Range #4,
will be conducted from 8 through 15 June. Tests to
determine compliance with contract specifications will
be conducted from dawn to dusk daily. Evaluations will
be accomplished by personnel of the 13th Army Ordnance
Division, Monmouth Artillery, Company B. Weapons systems of four Colonial Army contractors will be tested
at this time.

You are directed to deliver your 52C-3 Weapons System
and have it in place ready for transportation testing
by sunrise, 8 June.

Two field service representatives of your company are to be provided for maintenance supervision and training. Twenty-four sets of appropriate operating manuals and maintenance handbooks will be provided by the contractor.

You are advised that the highest level of security now in effect on the J2C-3 Weapons System must be maintained during transit to the evaluation site.

By Order of the Commanding Officer
Major Hollis Corby
Contracting Officer
J2C-3 Weapons Systems
Weapons Procurement Branch
Headquarters, Colonial Army
Philadelphia, Pennsylvania

HC:jb

cc to: Captain Earl Hawkins
Plant Representative
J2C-3 Contracts

FARNSWORTH
and
Cooper cannon and *Carriage Co.*

June 7, 1780
Salem Ordnance Plant
Salem, Massachusetts

Major Hollis Corby
Contracting Officer
T2C-3 Weapons Systems
Weapons Procurement Branch
Headquarters, Colonial Army
Philadelphia, Pennsylvania.

Dear Major Corby,

Leonard and I have the cannon down here ready for the tests. We sure think you will be pleased with the job we did.

We protected security on the cannon during the trip down, like you asked.

We built a box around the cannon the shape of a coffin and painted it black. Leonard and I both wore our black suits and we mounted a flag on the corner of the box. We polished the buckles on Hugo's (that's my horse) harness so he'd look good. We built a little bench to go on top of the box for us to ride on. When we pulled out of the shop in Wilfred Corners, the sheriff arrested us until we told him what was in the box. He said we'd been into so many troubles, he thought we might have shot someone.

As we drove through the villages on the way down here, people would remove their hats and stand in silence alongside the road. We told those who

asked that it was a war hero. Leonard and I think
it might be when it gets into battle. We're sure
anxious for the evaluation team to see how well it
shoots.

   We got to the testing grounds about noon
and have the cannon unpacked, all ready for the test.

    Sincerely,
    Andrew Farnsworth
    President & Project Officer
       T2C-3
    Farnsworth & Cooper Cannon
     & Carriage Company

Copy to Captain Hawkins
 Wilfred Corners, Massachusetts

FARNSWORTH
and
Cooper cannon and *Carriage Co.*

June 20, 1780
Salem Ordnance Plant
Salem, Massachusetts

Major Hollis Corby
Contracting Officer
T2C-3 Weapons Systems
Weapons Procurement Branch
Headquarters, Colonial Army
Philadelphia, Pennsylvania

Dear Major Corby,

  We are awful discouraged with the way things are going here. They still haven't started testing. They came out the morning you said they would and instead of "transportation testing," they began tearing our cannon apart.

  They said contractor supplied items must undergo complete dismantled inspection before being used by Federal Troops. Otherwise, they said, how would they know the cannon was safe to fire. We tried to explain how we'd fired it but they said if we did, we'd done wrong.

  They finished tearing our cannon apart yesterday and Leonard and I began putting it back together this morning. They said they didn't know how to put it together and that we didn't have any weapons system assembly manuals and that we should write some. They said we could do the writing while we put it together. They said Leonard and I had done it once and it should be easy for us.

      While Leonard fits the pieces together, I write down what he's doing and when he gets it all back in place, I'll have the manual all written. Leonard is kind of mad because he's doing all the work, but he doesn't write anything but his name so he sure can't write an assembly manual.

      The cannon should be back together, ready for the tests, in about two weeks of hard work. I'll let you know how we get along.

Sincerely,

Andrew Farnsworth

President and Project Officer

T2C-3

Farnsworth & Cooper Cannon

& Carriage Company

Copy to Captain Hawkins

   Wilfred Corners , Massachusetts

FARNSWORTH
and
Cooper cannon and *Carriage Co.*

August 18, 1780
Salem Ordnance Plant
Salem, Massachusetts

Major Hollis Corby
Contracting Officer
T2C-3 Weapons Systems
Weapons Procurement Branch
Headquarters, Colonial Army
Philadelphia, Pennsylvania

Dear Major Corby,

I just want to let you know how the tests are going. We got the cannon back together on July 5th. We were the first of the four contractors to finish reassembly so they started right in on the transportation tests.

Colonel Barton, who is in charge of Company B, Monmouth Artillery, got to talking with Leonard today and found out he's only 28 years old. He asked Leonard to see his draft card and Leonard didn't know what that was. They put Leonard in the stockade. I'd try to explain to Colonel Barton, but I don't have one either. Can you help me get Leonard out?

We've been working nights here in Salem, helping build a whaling schooner. We didn't bring supplies enough but for a week, so we had to get work to buy food. I guess Leonard will be fed now in the stockade.

They've been transportation testing the

cannon for about a month now. At first, they had trouble with the cannon because they didn't understand about how it is easier to push than to pull. After I explained about that, they were doing all right until Tuesday of this week. They had pulled the cannon through the Philo marsh on the west test range and to the top of Wilson's Ridge. They started down the other side and when they went to set the brake, they noticed we didn't put one on. The cannon got loose from the crew and smashed through a fishing shack at the bottom and then fell into the bay.

Colonel Barton said the accident was our fault because we should have put a brake on the cannon, so I'm repairing the fishing shack. It belongs to a fellow named Harley Toms. He was pretty nice about it. He helped me get Hugo (that's my horse) hooked to the cannon and we pulled that out of the bay.

I think they are going to start firing the cannon next week. I've been down here at the fishing shack days and at the whaling schooner nights so I don't know how the tests have gone this week.

I sold Hugo to Mr. Toms to pay for the lumber we needed to rebuild his fishing shack.

Sincerely,
Andrew Farnsworth
President and Project Officer
T2C-3
Farnsworth & Cooper Cannon
& Carriage Company

Copy to Captain Hawkins
Wilfred Corners, Massachusetts

57

FARNSWORTH
and
Cooper cannon and *Carriage Co.*

November 20, 1780
Salem Ordnance Plant
Salem, Massachusetts

Major Hollis Corby
Contracting Officer
T2C-3 Weapons Systems
Weapons Procurement Branch
Headquarters, Colonial Army
Philadelphia, Pennsylvania

Dear Major Corby:

Well, we got started firing the cannon yesterday. Your letter saying Leonard was exempt from the draft due to his critical occupation came Monday so he's been out of the stockade and helping get the cannon in place.

Everything was ready for firing yesterday morning. Colonel Barton had his whole Company out to watch. Leonard told them how to line it up to hit the target across the field about 400 yards, but they said they'd fired more cannons than we'd seen.

We knew there was going to be trouble with the way they set her, but we didn't know what.

The Colonel called some commands, "Attention. Unlimber piece. Secure side boxes. Advance sponge. Handle cartridge. Charge piece. Ram down cartridge." Leonard whispered that we were lucky to have fired the cannon without knowing all those words, but the Colonel hollered, "Silence," and then, "Fire," and it sure wasn't silent. She went off with a bang

I'll bet they heard back in Wilfred Corners.

We all walked down to the target, but Leonard and I were pretty sure we wouldn't find anything. Sure enough, the target was clean as a whistle. The Colonel stormed around looking for a furrow in the dirt where the ball hit. He said we were amateur cannonmakers and he never missed that far before and that something must be wrong with our cannon. I told him he should use the sight we'd built on the cannon, but he said a cannon wasn't like a musket and he didn't need a sight.

We came back up the range and he moved the cannon a little and yelled those orders again. She fired again just fine, but when we got down to the target, she was still clean.

The Colonel was really mad, but he couldn't figure out what was happening to his cannon balls. About that time, my friend, Harley Toms, came run-

ning across the ridge behind the target carrying
something and hollering his head off.

I knew before he got to us what he was saying because he sounded just like that hermit, Whippoorwill Green, when he hit his wheelbarrow.

Harley had a cannon ball in his hand with
grooves on it like our cannon makes. He said it
crashed into his fishing shack a half hour ago and
knocked it flat again. He was pretty mad and he swore
some at me when he saw me standing there. He said he
had that fishing shack for 40 years and that nothing
happened to it until I showed up.

Just about that time, Wakefield Harkins, who
I helped build the whaling schooner, came tearing over
the hill. He was dripping wet and swearing so he
didn't make sense.

When we got him calmed down, he said he'd
been finishing the cabin of his whaler when he heard

our second shot. About a second later, our cannon ball landed on the foredeck, plowed through two bulkheads and out the bottom, leaving a hole three feet across.

He said he tried to get it plugged, but the sea was coming in so fast he knew it was hopeless. But by the time he got on deck to put out his dinghy, the schooner turned on its side and sank right from under him. He had to swim ashore.

The Colonel didn't see how that could have happened, but he was so surprised that he listened while Leonard and I told him about our cannon and why we put the sight on it and how we'd hit Whippoorwill's wheelbarrow.

We all went back up to the cannon and Leonard and I lined it up with the sight and when we fired it, we could see the ball smash the target from where we were standing.

The Colonel was pretty happy about our cannon and invited Leonard and I to his headquarters where I'm writing this. He gave each of us a ration of rum, just like we were officers, and he said we could stay in his quarters until we complete the tests.

This was a good idea because Harley Toms and Mr. Harkins are outside the gate with their muskets and they said they were going to shoot me the first chance they get.

I'll write if we have any problems.
Sincerely,
Andrew Farnsworth
President and Project Officer
T2C-3
Farnsworth & Cooper Cannon &
Carriage Company

Copy to Captain Hawkins
Wilfred Corners, Massachusetts

62

FARNSWORTH
and
Cooper cannon and *Carriage Co.*

Major Hollis Corby
Contracting Officer
T2C-3 Weapons Systems
Weapons Procurement Branch
Headquarters, Colonial Army
Philadelphia, Pennsylvania

January 27, 1781
Wilfred Corners,
Massachusetts

Dear Major Corby:

      Leonard and I are back in Wilfred Corners.
The tests on the cannon were finished the first week
in December. Colonel Barton sent some of his troops
to help us rebuild the fishing shack. He reported
the sinking of the whaling schooner on a government
form for reporting ships sunk by shore batteries.
He didn't mention in the report that the shore
battery was our cannon. Anyway, Wakefield Harkins
is the only fisherman in Salem to have his boat sunk
and folks are looking up to him. So he forgave us
for the accident and said he'd about decided to re-
tire anyway. Colonel Barton said he wasn't sure, but
that he thought the government might put him on a
pension because of his record of naval service kind
of indicated he had seen action with the enemy on the
high seas. I guess Colonel Barton must have written
quite a few things into that report.

      Leonard and I set out to pull the cannon
back to Wilfred Corners by ourselves, but after a
day we'd only gone a mile and a half and we were
pretty tuckered out. We pulled the cannon back to

the Ordnance Plant the next day and Leonard and I talked Colonel Barton into selling us a surplus horse with a spavin. He said we could have him for $18 but we didn't have any money so we went to work in the Ordnance Plant until last week when we'd saved enough to pay for him.

He worked out fine and we got back with the cannon in just four days.

I want to get the cannon all cleaned up and ready to deliver and to get started setting up a way to build a lot of cannons at once cause we're sure you're going to like the report Colonel Barton wrote about how our cannon shoots. I sure want to get started because the winter has been pretty hard on the family here and the wife has had to take in mending and sewing enough to help out with buying the food. She couldn't hardly make enough to keep food on the table and sometimes had to get some on a kind of loan from the store down at the crossroads. Sure seems to take a lot to feed four children, then of course, Captain Hawkins was here, too.

Let us know what to do next because we want to go to work fast on more cannons.

Sincerely,
Andrew Farnsworth
President and Project Officer
T2C-3
Farnsworth & Cooper Cannon
& Carriage Company

Copy to Captain Hawkins

Colonial Army

30 March 1781
Philadelphia, Pennsylvania

Andrew Farnsworth
President
Farnsworth & Cooper Cannon & Carriage Company
Wilfred Corners, Massachusetts

In Reply,
Refer to: SRA-9877-16A

Dear Mr. Farnsworth:

The results of the Salem Ordnance Tests are being evaluated by the Weapons Systems Procurement Board (WSPB). Results of this analysis will be forwarded with recommendations, through channels for final review by the Congressional Weapons Committee (CWC), the Small Business Administration (SBA), and the Bureau of the Budget (BB). The finalized recommendations will then be submitted to the Secretary of Defense for final analysis and selection of the contractor for quantity procurement of 52C-3 Weapons Systems.

A renegotiation team will visit your plant late in April to review your performance on the 52C-3 Weapons System Prototype. They will inspect your accounting records and determine allowable costs for which you are to be reimbursed under contract. You are directed to have your 52C-3 Cannon ready for delivery by 1 May 1781. Necessary measures for insuring security during

transit will be taken. A unit from the Third Cannoneers of General Clark's Upper New York Brigade will be
in the Wilfred Corners area and will accept delivery
of your prototype cannon on behalf of the Colonial
Government.

By Order of the Commanding Officer
Major Hollis Corby
Contracting Officer
52C-3 Weapons Systems
Weapons Procurement Branch
Headquarters, Colonial Army
Philadelphia, Pennsylvania

HC:jb

cc to: Captain Earl Hawkins
       Plant Representative
       52C-3 Contracts

FARNSWORTH
and
Cooper cannon and *Carriage Co.*

June 1, 1781
Wilfred Corners,
Massachusetts

Major Hollis Corby
Contracting Officer
T2C-3 Weapons Systems
Weapons Procurement Branch
Headquarters, Colonial Army
Philadelphia, Pennsylvania

Dear Major Corby,

Sixteen Cannoneers from General Clark's Army came by on the 3rd of May and picked up our cannon. We had it all packed in a box for shipment so we could protect the secrets like you said we should, but they took the box off and pulled it right off down through town with nothing to hide it from everyone. They said they couldn't fight the British with their cannons in a box. They said the Redcoats weren't near so interested in how we built cannons as they were in which way we pointed them. They said that as soon as they could drag our cannon down to Maryland, they were going to point it at Redcoats. Leonard and I and our help, Corn-in-the-Woods, Red-Runner, Mose, and Mark Crossfield were all here and we cheered when they said that. Then they hauled the cannon off down the street and everyone in Wilfred Corners cheered and waved. It really looked good.

The renegotiation team you said you were sending was here last week. We told them all about how well the cannon worked, but they said they weren't interested in that. They said Leonard and I hadn't kept adequate records and that our expenses were unusual and extravagant. We told them we did everything just like you asked us to. They went around talking to our friends who loaned us money while we were building the cannon and some of them came to me kind of worried about their money. I told them you'd see we got paid all right and they didn't need to be worried.

       We're all ready to go into production on more cannons. Just let us know when to get started.

Sincerely,

Andrew Farnsworth
President and Program Director,
T2C-3
Farnsworth & Cooper Cannon &
Carriage Company

Copy to Captain Hawkins

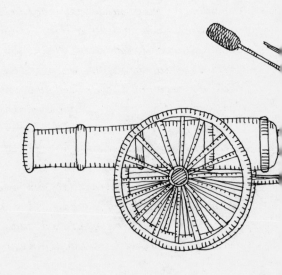

68

Colonial Army

10 July 1781
Philadelphia, Pennsylvania

Andrew Farnsworth
President
Farnsworth & Cooper Cannon & Carriage Company
Wilfred Corners, Massachusetts

In Reply,
Refer to: WPO 9473-A10

Dear Mr. Farnsworth:

I am pleased to advise you that the review of your
J2C-3 Prototype Weapons System produced under contract
with the Colonial Army has been completed and that the
performance of your weapons system in trials at the
Salem Ordnance Testing Center fully met the standards
of this program.

On the basis of this performance, a contract is now
being prepared under which your company will be asked
to build 100 J2C-3 Cannons for the Colonial Army.
Formal announcement of the contract may not be possi-
ble for some weeks, but as you know, the needs of the
Army are urgent and delivery under the impending con-

tract will be greatly accelerated. You are therefore advised that the Colonial Army Procurement Board finds it necessary to ask you to begin preparation for this contract during the interim period.

You will be notified when the conditions of the contract are determined and you will be asked to come to Philadelphia for the formal signing.

By Order of the Commanding Officer
Colonel Hollis Corby
Contracting Officer
52C-3 Weapons Systems
Weapons Procurement Branch
Headquarters, Colonial Army
Philadelphia, Pennsylvania

HC: jb

cc to: Captain Earl Hawkins
        Plant Representative
        52C-3 Contracts

FARNSWORTH
and
Cooper cannon and *Carriage Co.*

𝕳𝖊𝖓𝖗𝖞 𝕰𝖛𝖆𝖓𝖘 𝕮𝖆𝖗𝖗𝖎𝖆𝖌𝖊 𝕮𝖔.,
𝕬𝖘𝖘𝖔𝖈𝖎𝖆𝖙𝖊

August 30, 1781
Wilfred Corners,
Massachusetts

Colonel Hollis Corby
Contracting Officer
T2C-3 Weapons Systems
Weapons Procurement Branch
Headquarters, Colonial Army
Philadelphia, Pennsylvania

Dear Colonel Corby,

Congratulations on your promotion to Colonel.

Thank you for your letter advising us we won the contest and are to build more cannons. We went right to work as soon as we got your letter.

Leonard went down to Henry Evans Mill on Harness Creek west of town and talked him into adding on to his lumber mill. We plan to build the carriages for the cannons out there. Henry will get the earnings from the building of the carriages and Leonard and I will share earnings on the cannon itself. We're hauling all Leonard's tools out to the mill and are going to make Leonard's barn into another shop like mine so we can pour several cannons at a time.

We hired three local boys who just got out of the Army down by Boston and they are digging pits for our cannon reamers. Several fellows in town have offered to let us hire their horses to help with the reaming when we get started.

Captain Hawkins told us the security restrictions will be the same for the new contract so we've hired some more Indians for guards. They like to do that kind of work cause they can carry their bows and arrows and we make a badge for them to wear which makes them proud.

I sure hope the money comes for the prototype real soon. Ever since that renegotiation team was here, the people we owe have been coming around asking about their money every few days. We had to go over to Concord for a loan to begin the new contract since folks around here don't have much money left anymore. We had to give 10% interest over there.

We'll be ready to start pouring cannon barrels in about three weeks. Let us know if we have to get iron from the surplus depot like the last time as we want to get a supply up here before winter.

Sincerely,
Andrew Farnsworth
President and Program Director,
T2C-3
Farnsworth & Cooper Cannon Co.
Henry Evans Carriage Company,
Associate

Copy to Captain Hawkins

Surrender of Cornwallis at Yorktown.
(Photo: The Bettmann Archive, Inc.)

Colonial Army

24 September 1781
Philadelphia, Pennsylvania

Andrew Farnsworth
President
Farnsworth & Cooper Cannon Company
  Henry Evans Carriage Company, Associate
Wilfred Corners, Massachusetts

Dear Mr. Farnsworth:

You will have heard, by the time you receive this letter, of the notable victory of the Colonial Army at Yorktown and the surrender of the British Forces, under Cornwallis. The outcome of this battle has brought about the end of hostilities between the colonies and the British. Negotiations are now underway for final recognition of the Independence of the Colonies and a Treaty of Peace between our countries.

Naturally, the end of hostilities has ended the Colonial Army's requirements for weapons. You are advised that all contracts for weapons for the Colonial Army are hereby cancelled and declared null and void. This cancellation is made at the convenience of the Government under Public Law 188, "Convenience of the Government".

Inasmuch as your prototype contract was completed prior to the cancellation of contracts, your check for this work, $384.01 is enclosed. The Renegotiation Board found records kept by your company were not adequate to substantiate any payment for the contract. However, Government records of your purchase of iron from the Springfield Depot were located and determined to be satisfactory for reimbursement for that expense.

Since that amount was $375, you have been awarded earnings of 5% of that figure. Although this would be $18.75, 50% ($9.38) has been withheld and turned over to the Colonial Treasury as just payment of corporate income tax.

I am authorized by the Continental Congress to express the heartfelt thanks of that body, in behalf of the citizens of these United States, for the patriotic efforts of yourself and your employees during this long struggle for freedom.

By Order of the Commanding Officer
Colonel Hollis Corby
Weapons Procurement Branch
Headquarters, Colonial Army
Philadelphia, Pennsylvania

Encl: Check for $384.01

Post Office Department
United States Of America

11 April 1791
Philadelphia, Pennsylvania

Andrew Farnsworth
President
Farnsworth & Cooper Cannon Company
   Henry Evans Carriage Company, Associate
Wilfred Corners, Massachusetts

In Reply,
Refer to: USPR-88364-J-76

Dear Mr. Farnsworth:

In recognition of the role played by companies such as yours in serving as prime contractors for the Colonial Army during the War for Independence, the United States Government is now offering these companies the first opportunity to bid on a quantity of 300 postal wagons to be built for postal service in several of the nation's larger cities.

If your company is interested in bidding for this contract, please complete the enclosed bidders form (provided in triplicate) and return to this office not later than 15 June 1791.

By Authority of the Postmaster General
Directive Number 189

Malford Thomas

Malford Thomas, GS-11
Postal Service Procurement, Rm 1009
Federal Office Building #41
Philadelphia, Pennsylvania

Encl: Bidders Forms (3)

Post Office Department
United States Of America

7 August 1791

Subject: Bidder Solicitation Report

1.   Letter transmitted to Farnsworth & Cooper Cannon Company
returned. Recommend this be entered in Bidders Qualification Record

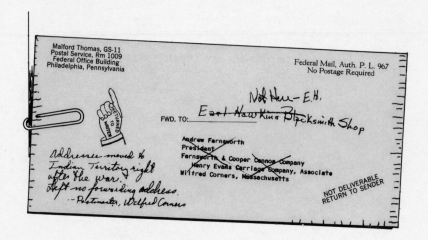

Malford Thomas, GS-11
Postal Service, Rm 1009
Federal Office Building
Philadelphia, Pennsylvania

Federal Mail, Auth. P. L. 967
No Postage Required

Not Here — E.H.

FWD. TO: ___Earl Hawkins Blacksmith Shop___

Andrew Farnsworth
President
Farnsworth & Cooper Cannon Company
Henry Evans Carriage Company, Associate
Wilfred Corners, Massachusetts

Addressee moved to
Indian Territory right
after the war. Left
left no forwarding address.
— Postmaster, Wilfred Corners

NOT DELIVERABLE
RETURN TO SENDER

"Lost time is never found again."

—Poor Richard's Almanac

"Those who expect to reap the blessings of freedom must, like men, undergo the fatigue of supporting it."

—Thomas Paine

"Indeed, I tremble for my country when I reflect that God is just."

—Thomas Jefferson

J. D. Thompson Publications, Inc.
205 W. Wacker Drive
Chicago, Illinois 60606

Gentlemen:

I would like to share with others the hilarity and the constructive critique of The "Free Enterprise Patriot"! Please send ____ copies ($1.50 each) to:

Name _____

Street Address _____

City _____ State _____ Zip Code _____

Enclosed is ☐ my check, ☐ money order in the amount of $____

J. D. Thompson Publications, Inc.
205 W. Wacker Drive
Chicago, Illinois 60606

Gentlemen:

I would like to share with others the hilarity and the constructive critique of The "Free Enterprise Patriot"! Please send ____ copies ($1.50 each) to:

Name _____

Street Address _____

City _____ State _____ Zip Code _____

Enclosed is ☐ my check, ☐ money order in the amount of $____

J. D. Thompson Publications, Inc.
205 W. Wacker Drive
Chicago, Illinois 60606

Gentlemen:

I would like to share with others the hilarity and the constructive critique of The "Free Enterprise Patriot"! Please send ____ copies ($1.50 each) to:

Name _____

Street Address _____

City _____ State _____ Zip Code _____

Enclosed is ☐ my check, ☐ money order in the amount of $____